flowers

COSMOS 10¢
KLONDYKE ORANGE FLARE

ROUDABUSH'S SEED STORE
Wilmington's Oldest Seed House
CORNER FRONT & DOCK STS. WILMINGTON, N.C.

flowers

20 jewelry and accessory designs

by Sian Hamilton

THE GUILD OF MASTER CRAFTSMAN PUBLICATIONS

First published 2014 by
Guild of Master Craftsman Publications Ltd
Castle Place, 166 High Street, Lewes,
East Sussex BN7 1XU

Text © Sian Hamilton, 2014
Copyright in the Work © GMC Publications Ltd, 2014

ISBN 978 1 86108 981 6

A catalog record for this book is available
from the British Library.

Set in King and Myriad
Color origination by GMC Reprographics
Printed and bound in China

Publisher Jonathan Bailey
Production Manager Jim Bulley
Managing Editor Gerrie Purcell
Senior Project Editor Wendy McAngus
Editor Nicola Hodgson
Managing Art Editor Gilda Pacitti
Photographer Andrew Perris

contents

Tools and equipment

Pliers and cutters — 8
Miscellaneous tools — 10

Materials

Embellishments — 14
Stringing materials — 16
Other essentials — 17
Findings — 18

Techniques

Findings — 22
Simple and wrapped loops — 24
Two-part epoxy resin clay — 26
Blanket stitch — 27

Continued...

MILLIE

PEONY

ROSE

ALICE

SHARI

MAGGIE

JEWEL

EMILY

DAISY

The Projects

Earrings
Millie	30
Peony	34
Alice	38
Shari	42

Necklaces
Jewel	48
Emily	52
Rose	56
Maggie	60

Bracelets & rings
Daisy	66
Olivia	70
Lauren	74
Sophie	78

Brooches & cufflinks
Lydia	84
Julia	88
Jem	92
Logan	96

Hair accessories
Hannah	102
Eden	106
Emma	110
Katie	114

OLIVIA

LAUREN

SOPHIE

LYDIA

JULIA

JEM

LOGAN

HANNAH

EDEN

EMMA

KATIE

Resources   118
Acknowledgments   118
About the author   119
Index   119

Tools and equipment

THE FOLLOWING PAGES SHOW THE COMMONLY USED TOOLS AND EQUIPMENT THAT YOU WILL NEED TO HAVE TO MAKE ALL THE PROJECTS IN THIS BOOK.

pliers and cutters

ROUND-NOSE PLIERS

These pliers have round jaws that taper to the end. They are used for making jumprings, eyepins, loops, and spirals.

CHAIN-NOSE PLIERS

Sometimes known as snipe-nose pliers, these pliers have flat jaws that taper at the end. They are useful for holding small items such as neck ends, and also for opening and closing jumprings.

CHAIN-NOSE PLIERS

ROUND-NOSE PLIERS

FLAT-NOSE PLIERS

These have flat jaws that do not taper. They are used for holding wire, closing ribbon crimps, and for opening and closing jumprings.

SIDE CUTTERS

These cutters have the cutting jaw on the side. They have a pointed nose and can cut flush to your piece. The point also allows the cutters to access smaller areas.

SCISSORS

Small, sharp, pointed scissors are used for trimming cords, ribbon, thread, and for cutting shrink plastic.

FLAT-NOSE PLIERS

SCISSORS

SIDE CUTTER

miscellaneous tools

ADHESIVE

When making jewelry, use glues that are suited to the purpose—many superglues can react with metals and melt materials. G-S Hypo Cement is a liquid glue that is good for adding to knots for extra security. E6000 is a thick industrial glue used to coat wire to stop sharp edges from scratching skin and for sticking shrink plastic to combs and metal findings. Use adhesives in a well-ventilated area.

TAPE MEASURE

A standard tape measure is an essential tool for measuring chain, cord, and ribbon, and for making sure the finished piece is the length you wanted.

TAPE MEASURE

ADHESIVE

PICK-AND-PLACE TOOL

This tool has a slightly sticky end for picking up and placing crystals or beads.

BEAD MAT

These mats feel like velvet and have a texture that holds on to beads, stopping them from rolling around on the worksurface.

MANDRELS

These are useful for making rings and bangles. They come in a variety of sizes and shapes, in both wood and metal.

BEAD MAT

MANDRELS

PICK-AND-PLACE TOOL

CUTTERS

Specialist cutters for polymer or resin clay are made from metal and come in a wide variety of shapes. Plastic sugar-craft cutters can be used; they are affordable and have a mechanism to push the clay out of the end.

SPACERS

Used to achieve a consistent thickness when rolling out clay, spacers are plastic bars that come in a set of different thicknesses. Using a stack of playing cards on either side of your clay works just as well.

SPACERS

CUTTERS

TEFLON SHEET

Sold in most cook stores, Teflon sheet is non-stick and is used to roll out clay on. It can be cut to size.

EMERY PAPER

This can be used to soften sharp edges on findings and wire or to smooth the edge of clay pieces. Specialist foam-backed emery paper holds its shape and works especially well on clay.

HOLE PUNCHES

Craft punches come in different sizes to cut holes out of fabric, paper, and shrink plastic. A standard stationery hole punch is a good size to use with shrink plastic.

HOLE PUNCHES

TEFLON SHEET

EMERY PAPER

Materials

Materials

embellishments

Be inspired by the huge variety of beads and charms that are available in a whole assortment of materials. Get creative by mixing up shapes, sizes, textures, and colors.

BEADS

There is a large selection of beads available, from tiny seed beads to large handmade lampwork glass ones. Beads can be made from plastic, wood, metal, glass, resin, or crystal. When choosing beads, it is good to start with a theme such as flowers, and then match different styles of beads together using a color theme.

CRYSTALS

Crystals come as beads, pendants, buttons, flat-back stones, and pointed-back stones, which are called chatons. They are beautiful and add sparkle to designs. Flat-back stones and chatons can be used with resin clay, or stuck on anything with appropriate glue.

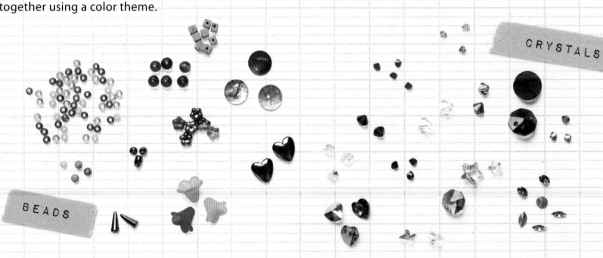

CRYSTALS

BEADS

BUTTONS

Shaped buttons are great for jewelry as they come with pre-made holes to attach them to jumprings or wire.

RESIN SHAPES

Flower shapes cast in resin come with flat backs for sticking to blanks, such as rings, cufflinks, or button backs.

RIBBON FLOWERS

Tiny ribbon flowers are available from haberdashers in many colors and styles.

POLYMER FLOWERS

Beautiful polymer flowers can be purchased in different sizes with a hole drilled through the base to attach them to jewelry findings.

BUTTONS

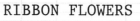

RIBBON FLOWERS

RESIN SHAPES

POLYMER FLOWERS

stringing materials

NYLON-COATED WIRE

There are a range of brands available. This wire is good for stringing, as it has a better strength for heavy beads than ordinary threads. It also holds a nice shape on the neck.

NYLON ILLUSION CORD

This thread does not stretch. It is called illusion because it is so fine beads look like they are floating when the piece is worn.

LEATHER, CORD, AND SUEDE

These come in various colors and thicknesses. They can be knotted with ease, or used with ribbon crimps or neck ends.

BEADING THREAD

Used with beading needles for seed beading. Thicker threads can be used for bead stringing and secured with calotte ends.

WIRE

Wire comes in a large range of sizes, usually measured by gauge in the USA and in millimeters in the UK. You can find conversion charts online. If you are buying plated wire, choose a non-tarnishing variety.

CHAIN

There are many styles and colors of chain available. Fine chains are good for hanging pendants, whereas large-link chains are good for making charm bracelets or when adding beads to the individual links.

NYLON-COATED WIRE

BEADING THREAD

WIRE

NYLON ILLUSION CORD

LEATHER, CORD, AND SUEDE

other essentials

SHRINK PLASTIC

This is a paper-thin plastic that shrinks in a standard oven and becomes seven times smaller and seven times thicker than the original size. It can be colored and cut into any shape with scissors. It also works with paper punches.

TWO-PART EPOXY RESIN CLAY

There are different brands of this clay available on the market; they all have slightly different working times but all dry naturally in the air. The clay comes in different colors and can be molded, modeled, rolled, and cut out. Crystal chatons (with pointed backs) will stick in the clay while soft without the need for glue. Other items can be glued to the clay after it has hardened.

SHRINK PLASTIC

CHAIN

TWO-PART EPOXY RESIN CLAY

findings

FINDINGS IS THE NAME GIVEN TO ALL THE OTHER ITEMS YOU USE TO MAKE UP JEWELRY SUCH AS JUMPRINGS AND CLASPS.

JUMPRINGS

A jumpring is a single ring of wire that is used to join pieces together. Jumprings come in almost every size you can think of and in many colors.

EARWIRES

Earwires come in various styles, from a simple U-shape with a loop to ones with a bead and coil finish. The loop is opened to take the earring piece.

HEADPINS AND EYEPINS

These are pieces of wire with a flat or ball end (headpin) or a loop at the end (eyepin). Thread a bead on the wire and make a loop at the open end to secure the bead in place. Eyepins can be linked together to make a chain.

POSTS AND BACKS

Posts come with a bead and open loop or with a blank disk front. The disk style is used with glue. These are often supplied with butterfly or scroll backs.

JUMPRINGS

EARWIRES

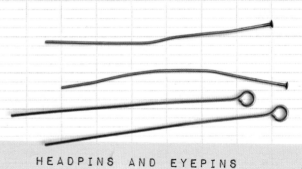

HEADPINS AND EYEPINS

POSTS AND BACKS

TRIGGER CLASPS

Also known as a lobster or parrot clasp, these are the most widely used clasps on the market. Some come with a jumpring attached and they vary in size and style.

MAGNETIC CLASPS

These are great for bracelets for anyone who finds opening and closing clasps difficult. Keep in mind that magnets will attach to some base metals, such as plated chains.

SCREW CLASPS

This type of clasp is best used with designs where the strung section can spin freely in the clasp, otherwise your piece will twist as you screw the ends together.

BOLT RINGS

These clasps are easy to use and have a spring-closing mechanism that pushes a bar across the opening.

BOX CLASPS

Available with one, two, or three eyes at the ends, these are great for multi-strung pieces. The lever piece pushes into the box and holds until the lever is pressed down again.

TOGGLES

This is a great choice when making the clasp a feature in your design. Toggles have a loop for one end and a bar that fits through the loop to attach to the other end.

TRIGGER CLASPS

BOLT RING

MAGNETIC CLASP

BOX CLASP

SCREW CLASPS

TOGGLE

RIBBON CRIMPS AND CORD ENDS

These are used to secure cord or ribbon. Ribbon crimps hinge from the top to trap the ribbon, while necklace/cord ends have side flaps that fold over the cord.

SIEVES

These are shallow domes of metal with holes that you can attach decorations to. Sieves come as rings, brooches, or plain to attach to jumprings. They often come with a domed backing plate with small hinges to attach the sieve.

HAIR COMBS

Clear combs can be used with wire and beads or you can glue a feature piece to the front.

BEAD CAPS

These are slightly domed shapes with a hole in the center and fit over the ends of beads as extra decoration.

BROOCH BARS

This is a brooch pin on a bar that has holes to attach it to the decorative piece you are making. It can be sewn on, attached with wire, or glued.

BEAD CAPS

BROOCH BAR

RIBBON CRIMPS AND CORD ENDS

SIEVES

HAIR COMB

HAIRBANDS OR TIARA BANDS

Round tiara bands can be used to sit on top of the head or gently bent out to make a U-shape for a hairband to sit behind the ears. They come in silver or gold colors and are made of a strip of metal.

BLANKS

These are items such as rings, cufflinks, or buttons that have a flat plate to which you can glue your decoration. You can get blanks on ring shanks, cufflinks, and as buttons.

HAIR BARRETTES

Plain metal barrette bases can be bought from many jewelry findings suppliers. They come in a variety of sizes and can be decorated with beads and wire or by gluing a piece on the top.

BEZEL BLANKS

These are flat plates in a variety of shapes with a shallow wall around the sides, so the surface can be filled with resin or clay. They either come with a loop to attach to a chain or are attached to cufflink backs, ring shanks, or bracelets.

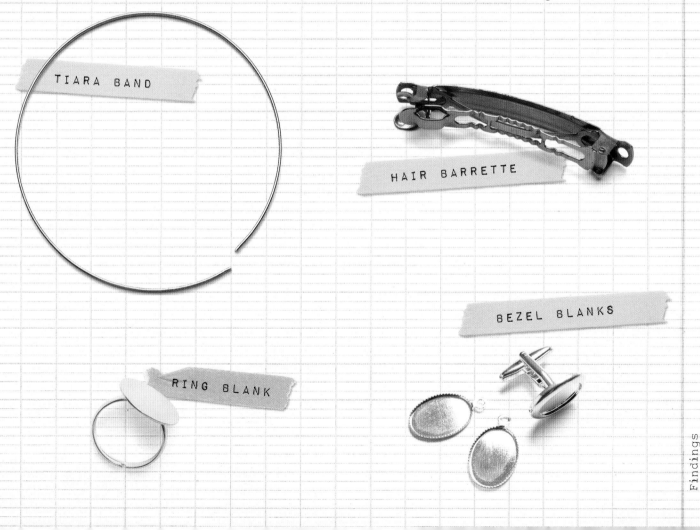

TIARA BAND

HAIR BARRETTE

BEZEL BLANKS

RING BLANK

Techniques

findings

Here is how to use and make some of the small components that make up your pieces of jewelry.

OPENING AND CLOSING JUMPRINGS

To make sure that jumprings shut securely, it is important to know how to open and close them correctly.

1 Grip the jumpring between two pairs of pliers. The opening should be centered at the top.

2 Twist one hand toward you and the other hand away—this will open the ring but keep it round. Reverse the action to close.

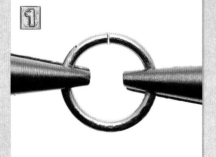
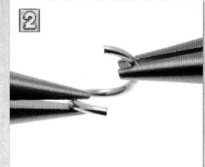

MAKING A SPIRAL

An attractive spiral works nicely to decorate pieces instead of using a simple headpin.

1 Take a length of wire and, with round-nose pliers, bend the very tip around in a loop.

2 Place the loop flat in the jaws of chain-nose pliers and push the wire against the loop.

3 Work round in a circle, moving the loop in the chain-nose pliers. Allow the wire to coil around the outside of the loop to make your spiral.

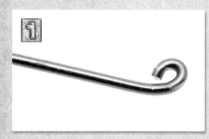

ATTACHING A CORD END

There are lots of different styles to choose from so pick one to complement the piece you are making.

1 Place the end of the cord level with the edge of the cord end by the loop. Using pliers, bend one edge against the cord.

2 Now press the opposite side over on top of the side that is already against the cord. Press the edge from the middle or it will not bend level.

3 Use the pliers to make sure the tube you have created is even and that the cord end looks neat. Finally, give a good squeeze to make sure the end is secure.

simple and wrapped loops

Loops have a multitude of functions in making jewelry
so making them properly is a skill worth mastering.

MAKING A SIMPLE LOOP

**A simple (sometimes called open) loop can be opened and closed to allow it to be attached
and detached as desired.**

1 Thread your chosen bead onto a headpin or eyepin.

2 Bend the wire to a right angle against the bead.

3 Snip off to ⁵/₁₆ in (8mm) or leave more wire if
   you need a big loop. Hold the end of the wire
   in round-nose pliers and roll back toward the bead
   to create the loop.

MAKING A WRAPPED LOOP

A wrapped or closed loop is very secure. Once an item has been attached this way it cannot be easily removed unless it is cut off.

1 Thread your chosen bead onto a headpin or eyepin.

2 Hold the pin against the bead with a pair of round-nose pliers and bend the wire above the pliers to a right angle.

3 Move the pliers to the top of the right angle and bend the wire all the way around the pliers until it sits by the bead.

4 Thread the loop onto the component you are attaching it to, such as a chain.

5 Hold the loop in the round-nose pliers' jaws with the chain away from the bead and wrap the end of the pin around the stem above the bead.

6 Wrap around until the wire meets the bead and snip off any excess wire.

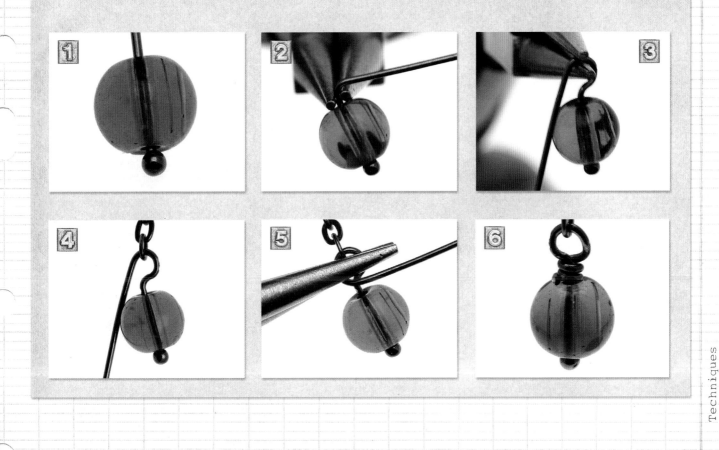

two-part epoxy resin clay

This clay is easy to use and can be fashioned into all sorts of shapes.

USING TWO-PART EPOXY RESIN CLAY

This clay is easy to mix and roll into a flat sheet. It can be cut and shaped and will stay soft for one to two hours, depending on the brand. Use only small amounts at a time because leftover clay will harden and not be usable again.

1 Roll equal-size pieces of both parts of the clay into balls. Make sure they are as close to the same size as possible. Mix for a few minutes to make sure the clays are well combined—if not mixed well enough, it will not harden. Most clays have one neutral-colored part and one colored part, which makes it easy to see if it has mixed properly.

2 Take a small amount of clay and place it on a Teflon sheet. Place playing cards or spacers either side of the clay and roll out with a roller until the sheet is an even thickness.

3 Cut your desired shape out and re-roll the rest of the clay to cut more shapes.

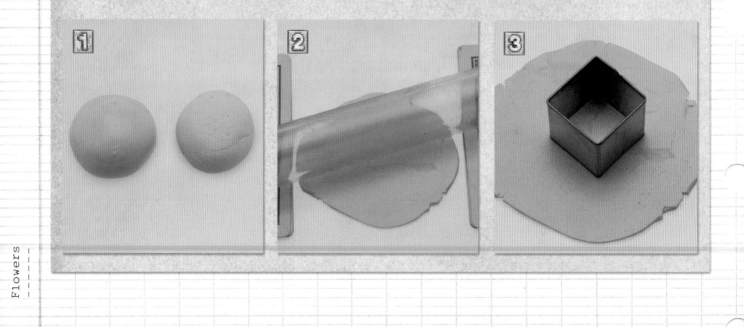

blanket stitch

This stitch is strong and decorative, making it perfect for edging and joining.

SEWING BLANKET STITCH

Any time you are using felt and sewing in a project, blanket stitch is a strong stitch to neaten an edge or to create folds for petals.

1 Thread a needle with thread about 18in (460mm) long and knot it at the end. Pull the needle through your felt about $\frac{1}{8}$in (3mm) down from the edge of the felt or fold. Pull the thread through to the knot.

2 Stay on the same side (opposite side to the knot) and push the needle through about $\frac{1}{8}$in (3mm) along from the first stitch, staying level. Loop the thread under the needle and pull gently, so the thread sits on the edge or fold of the felt.

3 Working from the same side the entire time, repeat step 2. Move along the fold or edge $\frac{1}{8}$in (3mm) each time, staying at a level of $\frac{1}{8}$in (3mm) down from the edge or fold. When you have finished the row of stitching, finish off with a double knot.

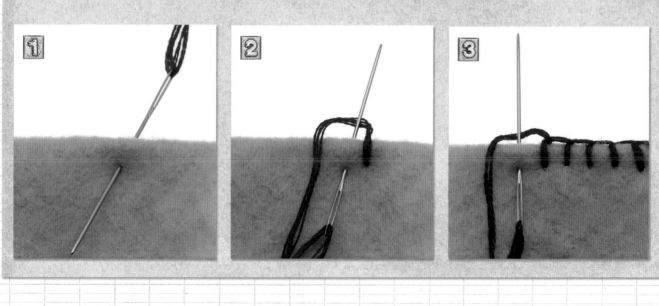

earrings

millie

These cheery, colorful earrings
bring a touch of spring.

Everything you will need...

Tiny flower beads clustered on chains are a simple way to make a lovely pair of earrings. Made with lots of different colors, you'll find they match everything.

1 x12

2 x24

3 x24

4 x24

5

1 12 x silver jumprings
2 24 x tiny plastic flowers
3 24 x clear seed beads
4 24 x silver headpins
5 2 x silver earwires
Round-nose pliers
Chain-nose pliers
Side cutters

Assembling millie

1 Take a headpin, a seed bead, and a flower bead. Thread the seed bead on the headpin first, followed by a flower bead.

2 Make a wrapped loop (see page 25). Make 24 flower pins in mixed colors.

3 Open a jumpring (see page 22), place two flower pins on it, and close the jumpring.

4 Take another jumpring, open it, place one flower pin, the jumpring with the flowers attached from the previous step, and another flower pin. Close the jumpring.

5 Following step 4, attach a row of six jumprings in total, with two flower pins attached to each jumpring. There should now be 12 flowers attached to the chain.

6 Before closing the sixth jumpring, add an earwire. Repeat this process to make the second earring using the remaining 12 flower pins.

TO MAKE THIS EARRING SIT NICELY YOU MUST HAVE ONE FLOWER PIN IN EITHER SIDE OF THE JUMPRINGS IN THE CHAIN AS YOU MAKE IT.

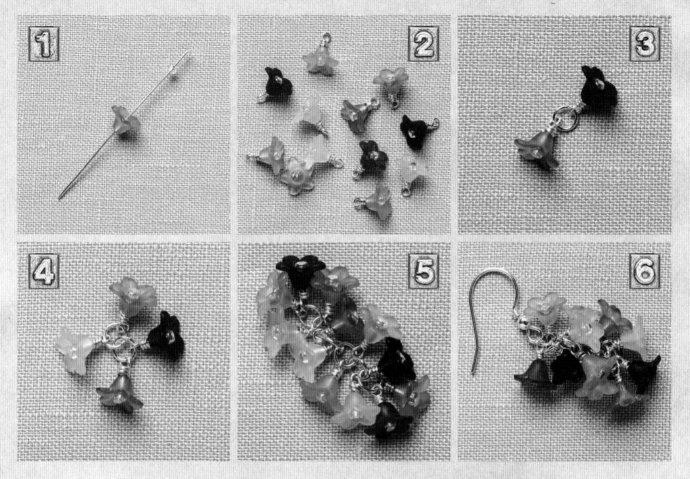

IF YOU FIND MAKING THE
WRAPPED LOOP A LITTLE
TRICKY YOU CAN USE THE SIMPLE
LOOP INSTEAD (SEE PAGE 24).

millie

peony

These classic earrings are right on
the button when it comes to style.

Everything you will need...

Covered buttons make great statement earrings.
You will find they are really simple to cover—you
just pick out your favorite floral fabric and get going.

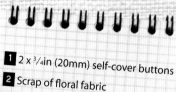

1 2 x ¾in (20mm) self-cover buttons

2 Scrap of floral fabric

3 Thread

4 2 x earring backs with flat pad

5 E6000 or similar strong glue

Needle

Scissors

Pliers

Assembling peony

1 Take the wire piece out of the button blanks by squeezing the loop bit with pliers.

2 Using the template that comes with the buttons, cut out two fabric circles.

3 Sew a tiny running stitch around the edge of the fabric circle.

4 Place the button on the fabric circle and pull the thread to gather the stitch around the button.

5 Check the front of the button to make sure the fabric is correctly placed.

6 Snap the button back into place and glue the earring back on top.

TRY TO FIND FLORAL FABRIC WITH A REALLY SMALL PATTERN OR USE WIDE FLORAL RIBBON INSTEAD.

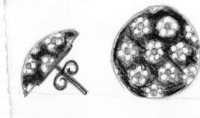

THESE BUTTONS CAN ALSO BE
PAINTED WITH METAL PAINT, OR DECOUPAGED
WITH PRETTY PAPERS. THE CHOICES
ARE ENDLESS!

peony

alice

These sweet paper and resin earrings
will add charm to any outfit.

Everything you will need...

Using pretty floral paper and a little resin, create cute earrings for the perfect day out. These are so quick and easy you can make a pair to match every mood.

1 2 x oval $\frac{5}{16}$ x $\frac{3}{8}$ in (8 x 10mm) bezel blanks

2 Small piece of floral paper

3 2 x silver earwires

Clear resin and hardener

Cocktail stick

Scissors

Chain-nose pliers

Assembling alice

1 On the flower paper, draw around the pendant twice with a pencil.

2 Then cut out the two shapes about 1mm inside the pencil line.

3 Cut out a few extra flowers.

4 Make up the clear resin to the manufacturer's instructions and lay the papers in the bottom of the blanks.

5 Add a layer of resin in each blank and then gently place in the extra flowers. Use a cocktail stick to move the flowers into the right position.

6 Leave the resin to dry completely. Attach the blanks to earwires to finish.

WHEN MIXING
THE RESIN STIR
VERY GENTLY TO
AVOID CREATING
BUBBLES.

Flowers

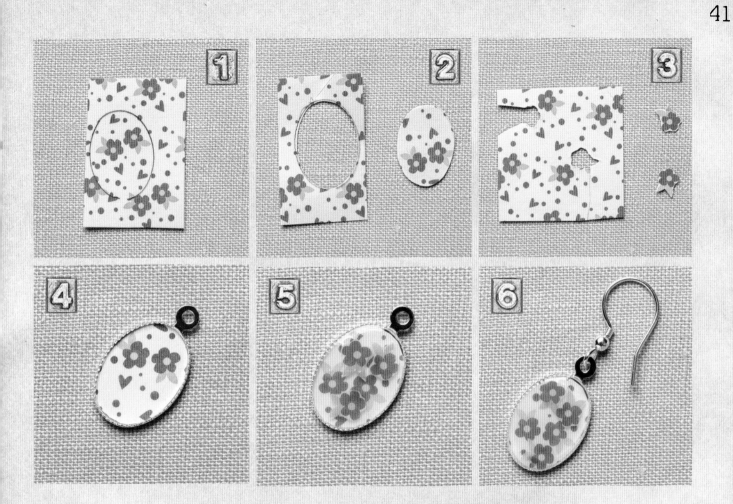

WHILE THE RESIN IS DRYING PUT
THE EARRINGS UNDER A CUP TO STOP
DUST GETTING STUCK TO THE SURFACE.

alice

shari

These stunning earrings
will spice up your day.

Everything you will need...

There are so many beautiful painted beads that feature flowers. These ones look gorgeous hung with a spiral and matching gold beads.

1 12in (305mm) length of US 22 gauge (SWG 23, 0.6mm) gold-colored wire

2 2 x large painted flower beads

3 4 x gold-colored bead caps

4 2 x gold-colored earwires

5 2 x size 8 gold seed beads

6 2 x size 6 gold seed beads

Chain-nose pliers

Round-nose pliers

Side cutters

shari

Assembling shari

1 Cut the 12in (305mm) piece of wire in half and make a spiral at one end on each piece (see page 23).

2 Thread on the size 8 seed bead, a bead cap, the large bead, a bead cap, and the size 6 seed bead.

3 Make a wrapped loop at the top of the wire (see page 25).

4 Open the loop on the earwire and add it to the wrapped loop.

5 Close the earwire loop to finish. Make the second earring in the same way.

AN ALTERNATIVE STYLE CAN BE MADE BY USING A HEADPIN INSTEAD OF THE SPIRAL WIRE. SIMPLY ADD ALL THE BEADS AND ATTACH TO AN EARWIRE.

THIS DESIGN ALSO WORKS WELL

MADE WITH A FLAT BEAD AND HUNG

ON A CHAIN AS A PENDANT.

shari

necklaces

jewel

Say it with flowers with this
fabulous statement piece.

Everything you will need...

This stunning four-tier necklace looks complicated but in fact it's very simple and fun to make. Just don't tell anyone that when the compliments start rolling in!

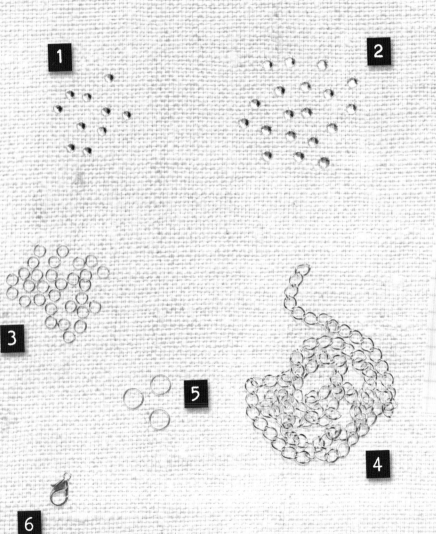

1 10 x ⁵/₃₂ in (4mm) flat-back clear crystals

2 20 x ³/₁₆ in (5mm) flat-back clear crystals

3 30 x 5mm silver-colored jumprings

4 26in (660mm) length of silver-colored medium curb chain

5 3 x 7mm silver-colored jumprings

6 Silver-colored clasp

Two-part white epoxy resin clay

Set of acrylic paints

G-S Hypo Cement (glue)

Talcum powder

2 pairs of chain-nose pliers

Pick-and-place tool

Roller

Non-stick surface (Teflon sheet or tile)

Flower cutters in three sizes

¹/₁₆ in (1.5mm) spacers (or playing cards)

2in (50mm) square of fine sandpaper

Needle

Assembling jewel

1 Prepare the resin clay according to the manufacturer's instructions (see page 26). When mixed and ready to use, roll out on a non-stick surface such as a ceramic tile or Teflon sheet. Use a little talcum powder to stop the clay sticking to the surface. Use $^1/_{16}$ in (1.5mm) spacers or a stack of three playing cards each side of the clay to roll the sheet out to approximately $^1/_{16}$ in (1.5mm) thick.

2 Take the three flower cutters and cut out ten flowers in each size.

3 Lay the flowers flat on the non-stick surface. Don't worry that they may be a little rough around the edges—you will clean them up when they are dry.

4 Take a sharp-pointed tool such as a needle and make a hole at the point of one petal of each flower. The hole needs to be big enough for a jumpring, so wiggle the needle around to enlarge the hole. This clay does not shrink, so the hole will remain whatever size you make it.

5 Leave the flowers to dry. Clean up the edges with sandpaper if they are rough. Then, using the acrylic paint in four colors, paint six flowers in each color, two in each size. Leave two of each size unpainted as white ones.

6 Now place a tiny dot of glue in the very center of each flower and place a crystal on top with the pick-and-place tool. Use $^5/_{32}$ in (4mm) crystals for the smallest flowers and $^3/_{16}$ in (5mm) for the other two sizes.

THESE FLOWERS COULD BE COLORED WITH PERMANENT MARKERS INSTEAD OF PAINT, OR YOU COULD LEAVE THEM WHITE FOR A WINTRY LOOK.

7 Attach 5mm jumprings to all of the flowers.

8 Cut the chain to four lengths: 14in (355mm), 16in (405mm), 18in (460mm), and 20in (510mm). Take a 7mm jumpring, open it (see page 22), and attach the ends of all the chains to the ring. Add the clasp and close the jumpring. With another 7mm jumpring, attach the other ends of all the chains and the one remaining closed 7mm jumpring.

9 Split the flowers into four groups, one for each chain. Use all sizes on each chain and mix up the colors. Starting with a large flower in the center of the shortest chain, add the flowers to the chain using the jumprings attached in step 7. You don't need to use all the flowers. Try the necklace on as you go and keep adding flowers until you are happy with how it looks.

emily

Cute as a button, this necklace is simple to make.

Everything you will need...

These cute, brightly colored flower buttons are combined to make a lovely necklace. Pick lots of jolly colors to add to the summery and playful feel.

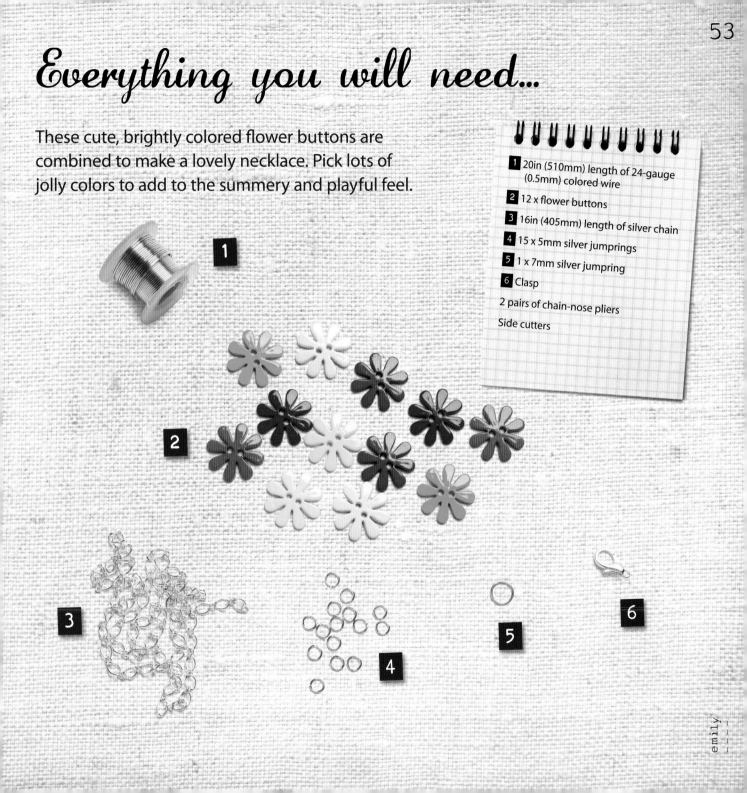

1 20in (510mm) length of 24-gauge (0.5mm) colored wire

2 12 x flower buttons

3 16in (405mm) length of silver chain

4 15 x 5mm silver jumprings

5 1 x 7mm silver jumpring

6 Clasp

2 pairs of chain-nose pliers

Side cutters

Assembling emily

1 Take the wire and thread on a button from the back through the front and to the back again. Place the button about 1¹/₂ in (40mm) along the wire, twist the two wires together, and cut off any excess wire on the short side.

2 Add another button, coming through from the back again. Push that button until it sits just over the one already attached. Bring the wire through to the back, then add a third button in the same way.

3 Take the wire through all three buttons again, to tie them securely together. The picture shows them from the back; from the front you should just see two wires going through each buttonhole.

4 Attach three more buttons in a row above the two added in step 2. Thread all three on and take the wire under a couple of the wires on the row below. Go back through the top row of three again to secure.

5 To secure the wire end, wrap it around one of the wires at the back and cut off neatly.

6 Take the other six buttons and link a 5mm jumpring onto opposite sides of each one. Place to one side, leaving the jumprings open.

7 Split your chain into eight equal lengths. With a 5mm jumpring, attach a piece of chain to the pendant.

8 Attach the other end of this chain to one of the open jumprings on a flower button. Close the ring. Attach the other chain to the other open ring on the same button. Repeat, attaching three buttons and four chain sections to each side of the pendant piece. Attach the final 5mm jumpring to one end of the chain and add the clasp before closing it. Attach the 7mm jumpring to the other end.

WIRING THE
PENDANT CAN BE
A LITTLE TRICKY
SO PAY CLOSE
ATTENTION TO THE
STEP IMAGES. USE
THE MAIN IMAGE TO
HELP YOU AS WELL.

rose

Hearts and flowers adorn this romantic choker.

Everything you will need...

Perfect for Valentine's Day or an anniversary date, this delightful choker is trimmed with ribbon roses and tiny heart buttons to give a sophisticated look.

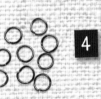

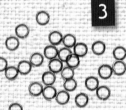

1. 5 x ribbon flowers
2. 4 x heart buttons
3. 30 x 5mm antique black jumprings
4. 9 x 7mm antique black jumprings
5. 2 x antique black neck ends
6. Antique black clasp
7. 14in (355mm) length of black cord

2 pairs of chain-nose pliers

Side cutters

Needle and thread

rose

Assembling rose

1 Take a ribbon rose and add a 5mm jumpring to each end (see page 22). Close the jumprings. Repeat for all five ribbon roses.

2 Take a button and attach a 7mm jumpring through both holes. Close the rings and attach both to a 5mm jumpring. Repeat for all four buttons.

3 Thread the roses onto the cord, going through the jumprings from the front so they sit on the cord as they appear in the step image. Thread on all five.

4 Take a 5mm jumpring and thread through the 5mm jumprings between two roses, attaching them together. Add a button before closing the ring.

5 Center the rose chain on the cord. To make sure it doesn't move when wearing, take a length of thread and sew the end jumprings to the cord.

6 Add a neck end to the ends of the cord (see page 23). Add four 5mm jumprings to each neck end. Add the clasp to the final 5mm on one side; add the final 7mm jumpring to the other side.

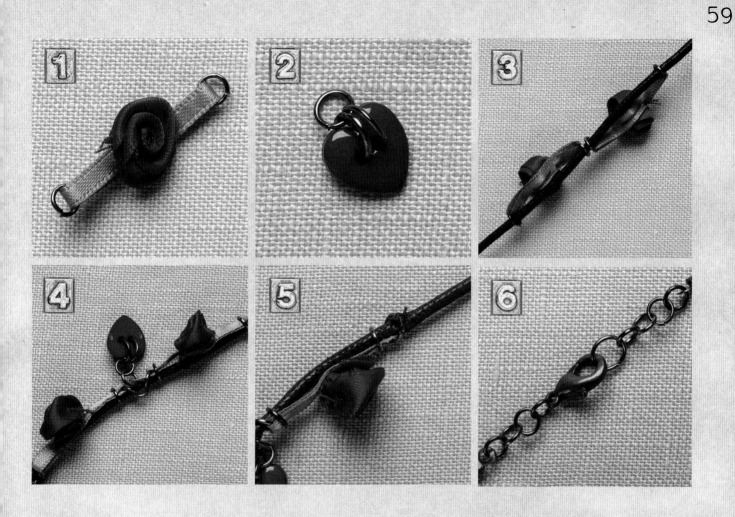

RIBBON ROSES COME IN ALL SORTS
OF COLORS. THIS NECKLACE WOULD LOOK
GREAT IN ANY COLOR BUT JUST MAKE
SURE YOU BUY ONES WITH RIBBON LOOPS
TO TAKE THE JUMPRINGS.

maggie

Square up to this pretty pendant, twinkling
enticingly with crystal decorations.

Everything you will need...

Making pendants out of air-dry clay is great for beginners. Adding crystals for a bit of sparkle makes a simple pendant stunning.

1. 10 x ⁵/₁₆ in (8mm) x ⁵/₃₂ in (4mm) peridot navette crystal chatons
2. 6 x ³/₁₆ in (5mm) fuchsia round crystal chatons
3. 60 x ⁵/₆₄ in (2mm) gold quartz round crystal chatons
4. 7 x 6mm silver jumprings
5. 2 x neck ends
6. Clasp
7. 16in (405mm) length of 1mm leather cord

Two-part epoxy resin clay

2 pairs of chain-nose pliers

Side cutters

Non-stick surface, such as Teflon sheet

Roller

Playing cards

Square cutters or a knife

⁵/₆₄ in (2mm) drinking straw

Pick-and-place tool

maggie

Assembling maggie

1 Mix the two-part epoxy clay to the manufacturer's instructions (see page 26). You will need about a 1in (25mm) diameter ball of each part to make this pendant.

2 Roll out the clay on a non-stick surface (see page 26). Use a small amount of talcum powder if the clay keeps sticking to the roller. Use a stack of ten playing cards on either side. Using square cutters or a knife, cut out three squares at 1¼in (32mm), 1in (25mm), and ¾in (20mm).

3 Gather the crystals. Using the pick-and-place tool, pick up a ³/₁₆in (5mm) fuchsia one. Start with the largest square and place the crystal on the clay; press down until the crystal is well embedded in the clay.

4 Continue to add crystals, using ten ⁵/₆₄in (2mm) gold quartz chatons for every flower. Make all the flowers first and add leaves around them.

5 Take the straw and make holes for the jumprings. Line the three squares up to make sure you have the holes level with the square above. The smallest square will need holes only at the top. Leave to dry for 24 hours.

6 Using the 6mm jumprings, attach the large 1½in (40mm) square to the medium 1in (25mm) one. Now attach the smallest ¾in (20mm) square below the medium square. Finally, add jumprings to the top of the large square.

7 Thread the pendant through the leather cord and attach neck ends to each end of the cord (see page 23). Using the 4mm jumpring, attach the clasp to one side. Using the last 6mm jumpring, attach it to the opposite side as the closing ring for the clasp.

TRY USING COLORED EPOXY CLAY WITH CLEAR CRYSTALS FOR AN ELEGANT FINISH.

Flowers

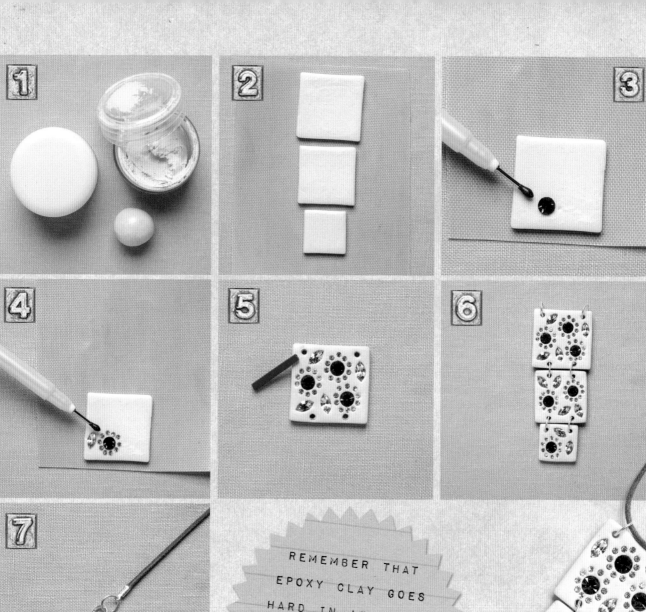

REMEMBER THAT
EPOXY CLAY GOES
HARD IN ABOUT AN
HOUR SO YOU WILL
NEED TO BE ORGANIZED
AND WORK SWIFTLY.

maggie

SHASTA DAISY
10¢

ROUDABUSH'S SEED STORE
Wilmington's Oldest Seedhouse
Corner FRONT & DOCK STS., WILMINGTON, N. C.

bracelets
& rings

daisy

Nothing says summer quite like a daisy chain.

Everything you will need...

Creating these pretty daisies in shrink plastic means
you can enjoy one of summer's pleasures all year round.
This permanent daisy chain is like perpetual sunshine.

1 Sheet of white shrink plastic

2 6 x leaf beads

3 18 x 5mm silver jumprings

4 1 x 8mm silver jumpring

5 Silver clasp

Pencil

Eraser

Yellow permanent marker

2 pairs of chain-nose pliers

Small hole punch

Scissors

x18

daisy

Assembling daisy

1 Take the sheet of shrink plastic and place it over the flower template (below). Using a pencil, trace six flowers on the matt side of the sheet.

2 Cut out the flowers. Then, using a small hole punch, punch out two holes at the positions marked on the template. Color the center of your flowers with a yellow permanent marker pen on both sides.

3 Use the eraser to make sure all pencil marks left on the flowers have been removed. Then shrink the flowers using the manufacturer's instructions.

4 Open six jumprings (see page 22) and attach them to the leaf beads. Open another ring and attach it to a flower plus a leaf bead. Open a further ring and attach it to another flower and the same leaf bead to start the chain.

5 Following step 4, attach a leaf bead in between each flower, using a separate jumpring for each piece. You should have a row of six flowers and five leaves with one leaf left over.

6 Add a jumpring to the clasp and then attach it to the flower end of the chain. Attach the final leaf bead to the other end of the chain and add your 8mm jumpring to the very end.

SHRINK PLASTIC COMES IN SOME LOVELY COLORS
SO THIS DESIGN IDEA COULD BE USED TO CREATE
A VARIETY OF FLOWER DESIGNS.

daisy

olivia

Masses of little flowers make
up this adorable bracelet.

Everything you will need...

Lots of sweet mini flowers threaded onto headpins with twinkling seed beads create an opulent cluster bracelet.

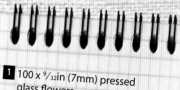

1 100 x ⁹/₃₂in (7mm) pressed glass flowers

2 200 x clear seed beads

3 100 x silver headpins

4 Bracelet chain with toggle clasp

Round-nose pliers

Chain-nose pliers

Side cutters

1

x100

2

3

x100

x200

4

olivia

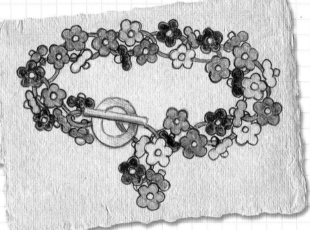

Assembling olivia

1 Take a headpin and thread the seed bead on it first, followed by a flower bead and another seed bead.

2 Make a simple loop (see page 24) large enough to fit on the chain link. Make 100 flower pins in the same way.

3 Open the loop on a pin to attach it to a link on the chain.

4 Place four or five pins on to each link.

5 Continue adding four or five pins to each link on the bracelet. You can add more if you want it to look really busy.

MIX UP THE COLORS FOR A
RAINBOW LOOK OR USE ALL THE SAME
COLOR BUT VARY THE TONE FOR
A MORE FORMAL STYLE.

olivia

lauren

Enjoy sparkle, glitz and envious
looks with this bling ring.

Everything you will need...

These gorgeous briolette beads are just perfect for making a beautiful show-stopping ring. Wire them onto a ring blank and you're all set to stun.

1. 5 x ⁷/₁₆ in (11mm) x ³/₈ in (10mm) flat briolette pendants
2. 1 x ⁵/₁₆ in (8mm) clear crystal bead
3. 16in (405mm) length of 26-gauge (0.4mm) silver-colored wire
4. Ring blank with flat pad

Side cutters

E6000 or other strong glue

lauren

Assembling lauren

1 Take the wire and thread on all five briolettes to the center of the wire. Bring the two wire ends together and twist them closed until all the briolettes sit together closely.

2 Bring the wires up in the middle and thread on the $5/16$ in (8mm) bead. Push the bead down until it sits centrally in the middle of the flower.

3 Take the wire ends through the middle again to the back. Opposite where the twisted wire section is, take one of the wire ends and bring it around the outside to the front and down through the middle again. This will catch the wire end around the wire running through the briolettes. Take the other wire end and do the same between another two briolettes.

4 Wrap the wire ends under the twisted section and around the back, catching under any wires you can see. Keep these wires facing in opposite ways.

5 Put a big blob of glue on the ring pad and stick the flower on in the center. Leave to dry. Finally, bring the two wires around and twist them around the ring shank a couple of times for extra security. Snip off any excess wire and add a tiny blob of glue to stick the ends down.

BE VERY CAREFUL WITH CRYSTALS—ESPECIALLY
THE ONES THAT HAVE STRAIGHT EDGES—AS
THEY CAN CHIP REALLY EASILY.

sophie

You'll have style at your fingertips
with this funky-colored bloom.

Everything you will need...

Large polymer flowers make eye-catching rings. This lime-colored one contrasts stylishly with the copper wire.

1 20in (510mm) x US 20 gauge (SWG 21, 0.8mm) copper wire

2 Large polymer flower bead

3 Ring mandrel

4 Chain-nose pliers

Side cutters

sophie

Assembling sophie

1 Thread the bead onto the wire and place it to sit in the middle of the wire. Bend the wire down each side of the bead.

2 Place on a ring mandrel and wrap both wires around once from opposite directions.

3 The two end wires should face in opposite directions. Wrap both around the base of the bead twice, in the same direction, so they always stay at opposite sides.

4 Take the ring off the mandrel and hold it firmly. Wrap the wire ends around the shank of the ring about four times.

5 Cut off any excess wire; make sure the cut end is on the outside of the ring shank. Using chain-nose pliers, push the cut ends against the ring shank.

TO PREVENT THE CUT ENDS CATCHING ON CLOTHES ADD A
LITTLE DROP OF THICK GLUE TO COAT THE CUT PIECE.

brooches & cufflinks

lydia

The perfect floral treat to embellish any coat.

Everything you will need...

With each petal made up of ten seed beads, this charming chrysanthemum brooch is quite fiddly to make but well worth the effort.

1 x900

1 Around 900 seed beads in four colors

2 1 ¼in (32mm) sieve-style brooch finding

3 Needle

4 Beading thread

Chain-nose pliers

Scissors

2

3

4

lydia

Assembling lydia

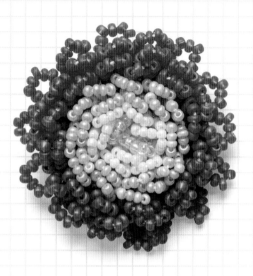

1 Thread a needle with a length of doubled thread and knot it at the back of the sieve through the center hole.

2 Bring the thread through the center hole to the front. Thread on ten seed beads in your chosen color for the middle. Take the thread back through the center hole.

3 At the back, take the needle under the thread a couple of times and bring it back through the center hole to the front.

4 Thread on another ten seed beads in the same color as in step 2. Take the thread back through the center hole.

5 Bring the needle back to the front through one of the holes next to the center hole. Thread on ten beads in the next color. Take the thread through the hole next to the one the thread came out of, creating a loop.

6 Continue around the sieve, making loops the same way as in step 5, until you have three loops. Then bring the thread through to the front using one of the holes on the next row out. Using the same technique, make a circle of six loops in this row.

7 Change to the next color seed bead and continue to make another two rows of loops in this color. Change to the final bead color for the outer petals. Start the row in the holes used for the previous color. Bring the thread from the back through the hole next to the one you have just finished. This hole will already have a loop in another color.

8 Make a circle of loops on this row. When complete, you will have two circles of loops on this row. Bring the thread to the front on the outer row of holes and do the same as in steps 7. Make two rows of loops on the outer circle of holes to finish.

9 To attach the back, place the sieve in the back plate and, using chain-nose pliers, push the tab over.

IF YOU ARE NOT SURE HOW TO FOLLOW THE STEPS AND EVERYTHING SEEMS A LITTLE CONFUSING REFER BACK TO THE MAIN PHOTO OF THE FINISHED PIECE TO SEE WHAT THE DESIGN SHOULD LOOK LIKE.

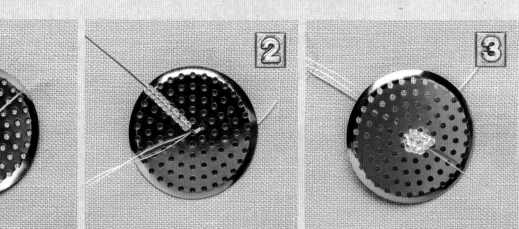

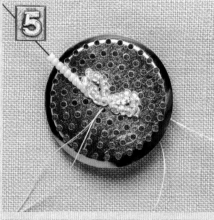

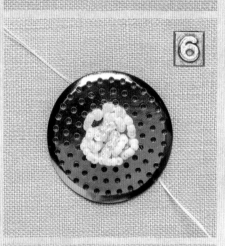

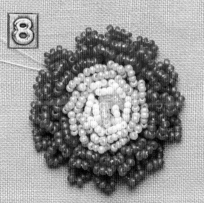

julia

Fabulously cute, this felt
brooch is sure to raise a smile.

Everything you will need...

Make a delightfully handmade statement with this fantastic felt flower brooch. Easy to sew, it is finished off with a pretty pearl button.

1 4 x 8in (100 x 202mm) of thin felt

2 1 x pearl button

3 Brooch pin

4 Thread to match the felt

Needle

Scissors

1

2

3

4

julia

Assembling julia

1 Cut out three flowers in felt using the templates below as guides.

2 Take the largest one and fold it in half with the opposing petals aligned. Sew a tight blanket stitch (see page 27) along the folded ridge, leaving $^5/_8$ in (15mm) open at both ends. Secure with a few small stitches.

3 Now refold the flower with two more opposing flower petals aligned. As you fold across the already stitched ridge it will get a little hard to sew —just stitch through the center. Refold for a third time and you should have a finished result that looks like the step image. Sew all three flower pieces in the same way.

4 Layer all three flowers together, aligning the largest and smallest ones and placing the middle one with the petals in between the other two.

5 From the back, sew through all the layers, securing them together. Sew through a few times without the button in the center, then position the button and sew through it a few times to secure.

6 Place the brooch pin on one of the sewn ridges at the back and sew on using the three holes in the brooch bar. Make sure it is well secured before knotting off the thread.

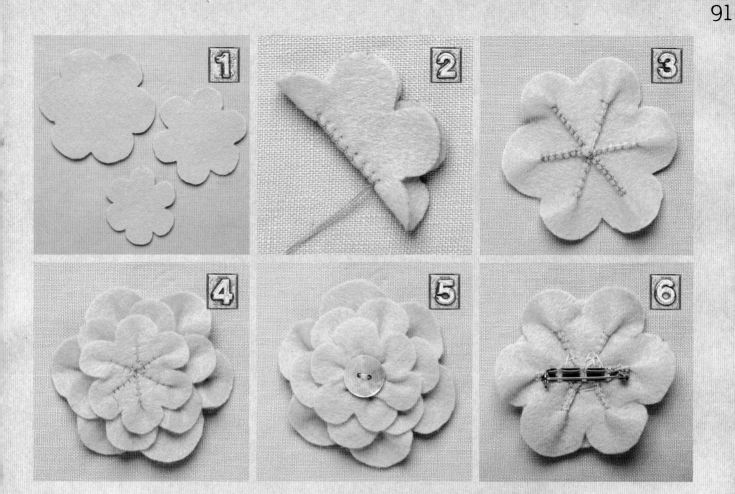

THIS FLOWER WOULD LOOK BRILLIANT SEWN ONTO
AN ALICE BAND OR ATTACHED TO A HAIR GRIP.

jem

Stylish and colorful, these cufflinks
are tailored to please.

Everything you will need...

The subtle floral design of these resin cufflinks
will brighten the wrists of any sharp dresser.
Simple, quick and fun to make.

1 Pair of cufflink deep bezel blanks

2 Deep pink and clear resin

3 Resin hardener

4 2 x flower shapes

5 Scraps polymer clay

Mixing cups and sticks

Jewelers' scales (optional)

Assembling jem

1 Prop both the cufflink blanks up with polymer clay. Make sure the tops are completely horizontal or the resin will not set level.

2 Mix up about $\frac{1}{32}$ oz (0.9g) of dark pink resin in a plastic cup. The ratio should be 2:1, resin to hardener. Count out 14 drops of resin and seven drops of hardener from the bottles. For extra accuracy you could use a plastic pipette or jewelers' scales.

3 Mix gently with a wooden stick to make sure no bubbles appear.

4 Place the flower shapes in the bottom of the cufflinks and pour pink resin over the top to the level of the flower, so the flower is sitting in pink resin but you can still see it clearly.

5 Cover the cufflinks with a cup to stop dust from settling in the resin and leave for 24 hours to dry completely.

6 Mix $\frac{1}{64}$ oz (0.6g) of clear resin by counting out 10 drops of resin and 5 drops of hardener. Pour it over the pink up to the level of the bezel. Cover with a plastic cup and leave to dry again.

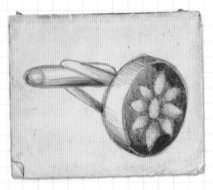

INSTEAD OF USING RESIN WHY NOT DECORATE THESE BLANKS WITH TWO-PART EPOXY RESIN CLAY AND CRYSTALS?

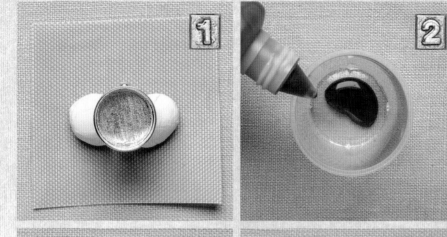

IF BUBBLES APPEAR IN THE RESIN, GENTLY WAVE A LIGHTER OR LIT MATCH ACROSS THE TOP. THE HEAT WILL MAKE THE BUBBLES RISE AND BURST. THIS SHOULD ONLY BE DONE WHEN THE RESIN IS WET AND ONLY BY AN ADULT.

jem

logan

These violet cufflinks have plenty of flower power.

Everything you will need...

There are many styles of flat-backed resin flowers in lots of gorgeous colors, so it's really easy to make a pair to go perfectly with any shirt.

1 4 x gilt button backs

2 2 x 6mm gilt jumprings

3 2 x 1⁵⁄₁₆in (23mm) flat-backed resin dahlias

4 2 x ¹⁄₂in (13mm) flat-backed resin dahlias

E6000 or other strong glue

2in (50mm) square sandpaper

2 pairs of chain-nose pliers

1

2

3

4

Assembling logan

1 Take the button backs and lightly sand the flat plate where the flowers will be glued. This will help the glue hold securely.

2 Place a blob of glue on the button backs and attach each one to the center of a flower. Leave to dry completely—E6000 glue dries in about an hour.

3 Using the chain-nose pliers, open a jumpring (see page 22) and attach to one of the loops on the back of a small dahlia.

4 Add one of the large dahlias.

5 Close the jumpring. Repeat for the other cufflink.

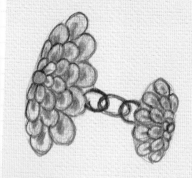

REMEMBER TO USE A SMALL FLOWER ON ONE SIDE AS THAT IS THE ONE THAT NEEDS TO FIT THROUGH THE BUTTONHOLE.

FLAT-BACKED FLOWERS COME IN A LARGE RANGE OF STYLES
AND COLORS BUT IF YOU CAN'T GET SMALL VERSIONS OF
THE FLOWER YOU WANT YOU COULD USE BUTTONS INSTEAD.

hair accessories

hannah

This gorgeous headband
is a cut above the rest.

Everything you will need...

Lovely beads are threaded onto wire to make the petals of this beautiful bloom. Perfect for any special event, this fantastic flower band is a head-turner.

1 1 x 32ft (10m) pack of US 22 gauge (SWG 23, 0.6mm) silver-plated wire

2 160 x ³/₁₆in (4mm) cats-eye beads

3 160 x size 6 (3.3mm) clear seed beads

4 Silver-colored alice band

Chain-nose pliers

Side cutters

Masking tape

E6000 or other strong glue

1

2 x160

3 x160

4

hannah

Assembling hannah

1 Take the wire out of the pack and unwind the ends, holding the coil tightly. Let the coil release gently in your hand. The wire will settle into a natural coil about 4–5in (100–125mm) across. Cut ten single rounds from this coil and bend each one in half using chain-nose pliers to create the bend. The shape should look like a thin petal and the ends should cross over.

2 Take one bent piece of wire and starting with a $^3/_{16}$in (4mm) bead thread on eight of them with a seed bead in between each one. Do the same on the other side of the petal, starting with a seed bead.

3 Push all the beads until the petal shape is tight, then twist the ends together. Twist for about $^3/_8$in (10mm). Make ten petals in this way.

4 Take five petals and straighten the end wires on each one so they sit straight down from the petal. Gather the five together and wrap a small piece of masking tape around the twisted wire base. Wrap it as tightly as possible.

5 Add in the other five petals around the masking tape; make them as even around the outside as possible. Wrap another piece of masking tape around this, using just enough to secure them.

6 Divide all the wires below the masking tape in half and bend out to a right angle on opposite sides. Now bend the petals out one by one to make a double-layer flower with five petals in each layer.

7 Cut a piece of US 22 gauge (SWG 23, 0.6mm) wire about 12in (305mm) long. Take the alice band and hold the flower against the band about one-third of the way up on one side. Lay the flower on the band with the wires running along the band and hold the flower and band together with one hand. Take the piece of wire and wrap around the wires and band, starting about $^1/_2$in (12mm) from the flower stem. Wrap to the stem, bring the wire under the stem, and wrap for $^1/_2$in (12mm) down the other side. Cut off any excess wire.

8 Cut off all of the wire ends at the end of the coils using the side cutters with the flush side against the wrapped end. Be careful of flying wires—try to hold the wires in one hand and use the cutters in the other hand.

9 To finish, wrap a section of wire around the stem of the flower to cover the masking tape. To make all the wire ends safe, use a cocktail stick and coat with a tiny amount of E6000 glue. Bend petals into shape.

THIS FLOWER WOULD LOOK GREAT MADE IN
CRYSTALS FOR A BRIDESMAID'S TIARA.

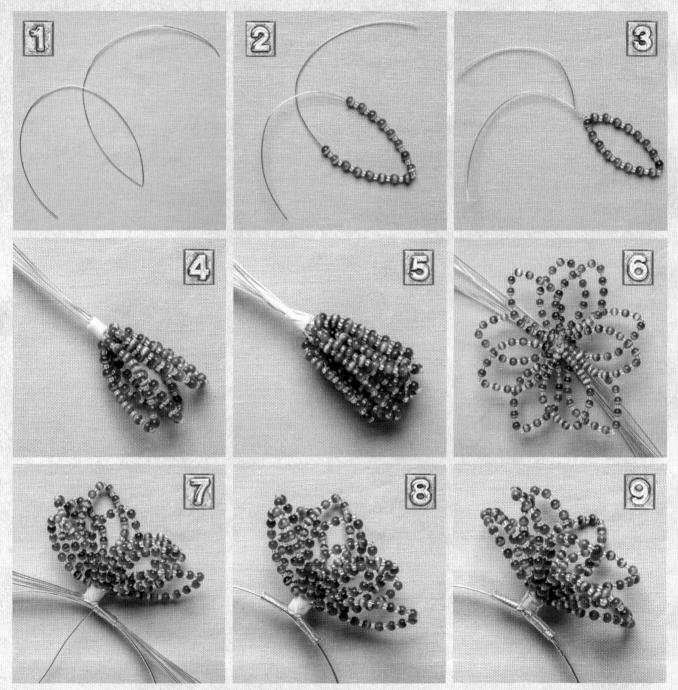

eden

Rainbow-colored flower clusters
adorn this beautiful barrette.

Everything you will need...

Clusters of flowers and beads are secured with wire to a barrette to make a pretty hair clip that would suit any occasion.

1. 2¹/₂in (60mm) silver-colored barrette
2. 18 x tiny plastic flowers
3. 30 x size 6 (3.3mm) seed beads in blue, pink, pastel blue, gold, and turquoise
4. 80in (2m) length of US 26 gauge (SWG 27, 0.4mm) silver-colored wire

Side cutters

eden

Assembling eden

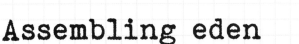

1 Separate the back of the barrette from the front to make it easier to use. To do this, push against one side holding the back piece in—it will pop out easily. The middle spring piece will then fall out too. Keep these safe!

2 Cut a 16in (405mm) piece of US 26 gauge (SWG 27, 0.4mm) wire. It will be easier to work with short sections of wire, but cut a longer piece if preferred. Thread the wire through the hole at one end of the front piece. Fold the wire back to meet itself and twist to secure it in place.

3 Wrap the twisted wire end around the barrette end and bring the wire through the hole from the back. This has secured the wire neatly and you can now start adding beads.

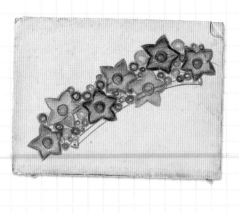

4 Take a flower and thread on to the wire, then add a seed bead in a contrasting color. Take the wire back through the flower bead, around the outside of the seed bead. Holding the flower bead against the barrette, pull the wire until the bead is tight against the flower, with the flower sitting tight against the barrette.

5 Wrap the wire around the barrette bar once and add another flower and bead in different colors. Add a third flower and bead in the same way. Remember to hold the flower tightly as you pull the wire through to secure the bead and always wrap the wire around the barrette bar again afterwards to secure.

6 When you have secured the third flower, push the trio to the end of the barrette and wrap the wire around the end twice. Thread on three seed beads in different colors and wrap around the barrette. Take the wire around again to secure. Add another row of three seed beads and wrap the wire around the bar.

7 Now add the next three flowers in the same way as the first three, adding one at a time with a wrap of wire around the barrette bar to secure. Add the next three seed beads and wrap the wire around the barrette again. You may run out of wire here. When you do, just wrap the end around the barrette as many times as it will fit, then cut a new piece and wrap that around the barrette a couple of times as well.

8 Continue using the same steps to add two rows of beads then three flowers until you reach the end of the barrette bar. When you get to the final two rows of seed beads, wrap any remaining wire around the bar.

9 Start with a new piece of wire and repeat step 1 to attach the last three flowers to the end. Wrap the wire around the bar at the end and snip off any excess wire, tucking the end underneath a flower. Add a little glue to the end to make sure the wire doesn't come undone. Finally, place the back of the barrette clip in place.

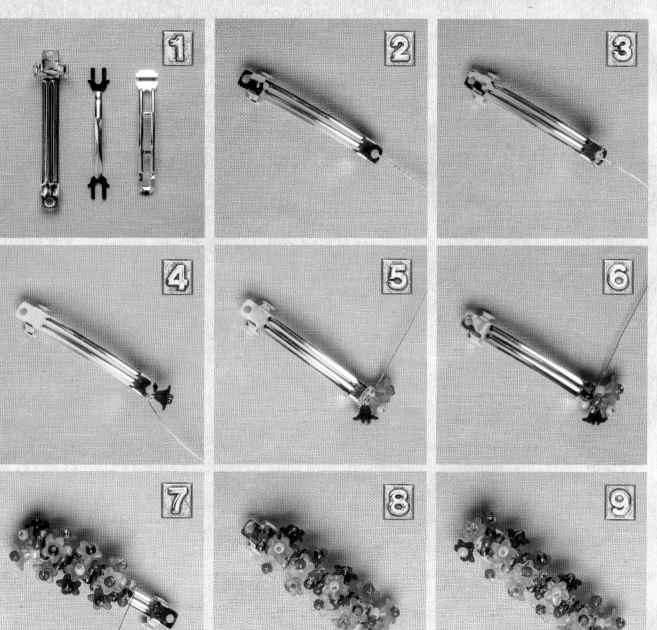

emma

A jaunty hair grip, perfect for a summer party.

Everything you will need...

Pretty flowers and beautiful beads attached to a hair grip by lengths of chain create a delightful decoration that is as fun to wear as it is to make.

1. 12 x small plastic flowers
2. 12 x ³/₁₆ in (4mm) antique copper metal beads
3. 12 x 1⁹/₁₆ in (40mm) copper headpins
4. 16in (405mm) length of antique copper fine chain
5. 12in (305mm) length of US 26 gauge (SWG 27, 0.4mm) copper wire
6. Hair grip

Round-nose pliers

Side cutters

Flat-nose pliers

Assembling emma

1 Thread a copper bead then a flower onto a headpin. Make five more.

2 Start to make a wrapped loop (see page 25), but before you finish the loop, open it slightly and thread on a 3¹/₂ in (90mm) length of chain. Finish the wrapped loop. Repeat for the other five headpins, attaching to chains reducing in length by ³/₈ in (10mm) each time.

3 Make up the other six flowers in the same way but don't add any chain. Place to one side.

4 Take the US 26 gauge (SWG 27, 0.4mm) wire and place it on the hair grip. Twist the ends together to secure the wire.

5 Thread on all six chains and twist the wire around the end of the grip to secure the chains.

6 Thread on a flower made in step 3 and twist the wire around the grip again. Go through the loop of the flower twice to hold it in place. Add another flower and do the same. Add a third flower and wrap the wire around all three flowers to hold them securely. Add the other three flowers around the outside, wrapping the wire around a couple of times in between adding the flowers. Finish by wrapping the wire around the hair grip a couple of times and cut off any excess.

AN ALTERNATIVE DESIGN WOULD BE
TO MAKE A BIGGER CLUSTER ON THE GRIP
WITHOUT ANY HANGING CHAINS.

katie

This blooming marvelous
hair slide is sure to
brighten your day.

Everything you will need...

Shrink plastic is a great material to experiment with. The possibilities are endless and it works really well for both children's and adults' accessories.

1 10 ½ x 8in (262 x 202mm) sheet of frosted shrink plastic

2 2 ¾ in (70mm) clear comb

3 Pencil

4 Colored pencils in bright yellow, bright pink, white, orange, bright green, and dark green

E6000 glue

Scissors

katie

Assembling katie

1 Using the template provided, draw the flower shape on the matt side of the shrink plastic. You will be able to see through the frosted plastic so place it on top of the template and trace the outline. Use the yellow pencil to draw the circle in the center and the white pencil to draw the petals. Draw three. Use the bright green pencil to draw three leaf shapes.

2 Cut roughly around each shape. Using the template to see where each color goes, start with the center of the flowers and color them in with bright yellow and then shade half the circle with orange.

3 Color in the petals with white (this will be easier if you place the plastic over a darker color so you can see the white pencil line). Then, using a pink pencil, draw lines out from the center circle. With the longest line in the center of each petal, make shorter lines out toward the edges of the petals.

4 Color in the leaves with bright green. Then go over the edges with darker green and draw in lines from the center. Use the photograph as a guide.

5 Cut out all the pieces. Be careful, as shrink plastic can tear easily. Shrink in a domestic oven using the manufacturer's instructions. Always watch the plastic as it shrinks really quickly and can melt if left in the oven for too long. As you take the pieces out of the oven, before they completely cool, lay the flowers face down over a dome shape, such as a light bulb. This is optional as the flowers would look fine flat as well.

6 Let all the pieces cool. Then, using the E6000 glue, stick the three flowers in a line across the top of the comb. Place them so the petals overlap, then glue the leaves in behind the flowers.

SHRINK PLASTIC COMES IN PACKS WITH
DIFFERENT FLOWERS ALREADY PRINTED ON
THAT JUST NEED COLORING IN. THIS
WOULD WORK WELL IF YOU ARE MAKING
THIS PROJECT WITH A CHILD.

katie

resources

SOURCES OF MATERIALS

UK

Beads Unlimited
PO Box 1
Hove
East Sussex
BN3 5SG
Tel: +44 (0)1273 740777
www.beadsunlimited.co.uk

Beads Direct Ltd
10 Duke Street
Loughborough
Leicestershire
LE11 1ED
Tel: +44 (0)1509 218028
www.beadsdirect.co.uk

The Bead Shop
44 Higher Ardwick
Manchester
M12 6DA
Tel: +44 (0)161 274 4040
www.the-beadshop.co.uk

Fred Aldous Ltd
37 Lever Street
Manchester
M1 1LW
Tel: +44 (0)161 236 4224
www.fredaldous.co.uk

Bead and Button Company
The Workshop
58 Lower North Road
Carnforth
Lancashire
LA5 9LJ
www.beadandbuttoncompany.co.uk

Palmer Metals Ltd
401 Broad Lane
Coventry
CV5 7AY
Tel: +44 (0)845 644 9343
www.palmermetals.co.uk

Spoilt Rotten Beads
7 The Green
Haddenham
Ely
Cambridgeshire
CB6 3TA
Tel: +44 (0)1353 749853
www.spoiltrottenbeads.co.uk

Jillybeads
1 Anstable Road
Morecambe
LA4 6TG
Tel: +44 (0)1524 412728
www.jillybeads.co.uk

USA

Fire Mountain Gems and Beads
1 Fire Mountain Way
Grants Pass
OR 97526-2373
Tel: toll free 1-800-355-2137
Tel: from UK 1-541-956-7890
www.firemountaingems.com

acknowledgments

I would like to thank Tansy Wilson for her guidance on writing my first book, and my husband Tony for his patience in allowing me to take up weekends to write this book. I would also like to thank the GMC Publications team for making it an easy ride.

ADDITIONAL PHOTOGRAPHY CREDITS

Florida Memory: 244994 (p120 center left, p46 center right); JJS0361A (p5 top right, p100 top left); JJS0466 (p1 top right, p28 bottom left); JJS2156 (p3 center left, p101 top center).

George Eastman House: 1974 0238 0086 (p2 top center); 1978 0170 0004 (p65 center right); 2008 0502 0009 0001 (p65 photo frame); 2008 0503 0016 0001 (p5 bottom right, p47 center); 2008 0503 0014 0001 (p2 top left, p64 center left); 2008 0501 0013 0001 (p82 bottom right, p120 center left).

OSU Special Collections & Archives: P 009 P 075 (p46 top center).

Powerhouse Museum: Gift of Elizabeth Bullard, 1967 (p47 bottom right, p120 center right).

Smithsonian Institution: JJS0466 (p28 center).

The Library of Congress: LC-B2-2563-4 (p3 top left, p65 center left); LC-USW36-858_Collier (p100 bottom right).

The U.S. National Archive: 412-DA-10591 (p1 bottom left, p82 top left); 412-DA-3208 (p101 center, p118 center right); 412-DA-7978 (p3 bottom right); 412-DA-7979 (p2 bottom left, p29 center).

about the author

Sian Hamilton graduated from Brighton University in the southeast of England with a BA Honors Degree in Three-dimensional Design. She has worked in the design industry for more than 20 years, working mainly in ceramics and jewelry design. Sian is currently the editor of *Making Jewellery* magazine alongside running her own jewelry company making wedding accessories and bespoke jewelry for private clients.

index

A
adhesive 10
Alice 38-41

B
beads 14
bead caps 20
   mat 11
blanks 20
blanket stitch 27
bolt rings 19
brooch bars 20
buttons 15

C
chain-nose pliers 8
clasps 19
cord, 16
   end, attaching a, 23
crystals 14
cutters 12

D
Daisy 66-69

E
earwires 18
Eden 106-109
emery paper 13
Emily 52-55
Emma 110-113
epoxy resin clay 17, 26
eyepins 18

F
flat-nose pliers 9

H
hairbands 21
hair barrettes 20
hair combs 20
Hannah 102-105
headpins 18
hole punches 13

J
Jem 92-95
Jewel 48-51
Julia 88-91
jumprings 18, 22

K
Katie 114-117

L
Lauren 74-77
Logan 96-99
loop, simple 24
   wrapped 25
Lydia 84-87

M
Maggie 60-63
mandrels 11
Millie 30-33

O
Olivia 70-73

P
Peony 34-37
pick-and-place tool 11
pliers 8-10
polymer flowers 15
posts and backs 18

R
resin shapes 15
ribbon flowers 15
ribbon crimps and
   cord ends 20
Rose 56-59
round-nose pliers 8

S
scissors 9
Shari 42-45
shrink plastic 17
side cutter 9
sieve 20
Sophie 78-81
spacers 12
spiral, making 23
stringing materials 16

T
tape measure 10
Teflon sheet 13
tiara bands 21
toggles 19

To place an order, or request
a catalog, contact:

GMC Publications Ltd
Castle Place, 166 High Street,
Lewes, East Sussex, BN7 1XU
United Kingdom

Tel: +44 (0)1273 488005

www.gmcbooks.com